Making It Without Mom

Reclaiming Your Power Over the Pain

After Losing Your Mom

Dr. Shauntel Peak-Jimenez

ISBN-13: 978-1511473422

ISBN-10: 1511473428

This book is not meant to replace any professional or medical advice. It is meant as a spiritual resource to inspire you forward on your journey of healing and restoration, related to your mom passing away.

Dedication

This book is dedicated to my sister Sherry and my brother Greg. I know that Mama would be so proud of us all. We had a wonderful mother and because of what she instilled in us, her light continues to shine bright. This journey without Mama has not been easy, but together we made it. I love you both so much and I am blessed to be your sister.

This book is also dedicated to my best friend Sheila Clark-Johnson. I wanted to dedicate this book to you, too, because I know you are also making it without your mom. She would be so proud of you.

This book is also dedicated to all of the other amazingly strong individuals who are making it without their moms. May God and the beautiful memory of your mother continue to give you an abundance of strength and comfort.

Acknowledgements

I am thankful to God for giving me the strength to persevere through the pain of losing my mom. And thank you to my encouraging, loving, and supportive family and friends. I appreciate all of you for helping me to continue to go on when I wanted to give up. Because of your love and commitment to me, I made it. I am grateful to you beyond words. You are a blessing to my life.

Contents

Introduction

In a picture perfect world, our moms would live here on earth with us forever. In a picture perfect world, there would be no pain, sadness, or tears related to a mom passing. But as we know, that is not the case. My mother was the heartbeat of who I am. She was my greatest fan, my strength, my joy, and my rock. And I just could not ever imagine my life without her. No matter what I did in life, she encouraged me, she supported, me and she believed in me.

I will never forget the day I received the call that changed my life. I was standing in Walmart in the line, and I received a phone call that I had to get to the hospital immediately. My heart just knew that it was my mother. I felt that it was my mother because it was odd that she wasn't the one calling me, but it was my sister on the phone. I immediately asked, "What's wrong with Mama?" I heard some machines beeping in the background, so I thought maybe she had an accident or something.

I vaguely remember the drive to the hospital. But I do remember not stopping for any lights. By the time I got to the hospital, I saw a few other family members coming as well. They were all sobbing and looking devastated. I frantically ran thorough the hospital looking for my sister. I was led into the room where she was at with a doctor and a chaplain. She, along with the chaplain, told me that my mom had passed away suddenly. We found out later that she had a blood clot.

When I found out my mom passed away, I immediately felt my stomach drop to my knees. I felt so many mixed emotions as I tried to comprehend what I was told. As I saw my mom's lifeless body lying in that emergency room bed, I literally felt my mind snap and my heart crumble. My mind and heart went somewhere they had never been before, and it was a feeling I will never forget. My whole world was turned upside down in a matter of a few minutes. One minute my mom was here, and then in an instant she wasn't. It was surreal to me, and I just couldn't make sense of what was happening to me. My mind couldn't grasp that my mom was gone, and I don't think my mind really grasped it until she didn't call me on the phone the next day, or show up to the next family event.

My mom passing away was a tough time for me, but a moment of celebration for her as she began her new life with the Lord. There is no greater comfort to me today than knowing my mom is in the presence of the Lord. She worked diligently all of her life to go to heaven, and she made it. That is a blessing. My mom only departed from this earthly realm, but she transitioned to the spiritual realm, one that I couldn't see, but one that I had to learn how to feel through my heart and soul. But that is something that took a lot of faith, a lot of time, and a lot of patience.

A mother passing away is never easy. One of the hardest things I have ever faced in my life was the passing of my mother. It hurt beyond anything that words can describe. The gripping pain seemed to rip my heart out and crush my soul. My 51 year old mother passed away unexpectedly in 2001, two days after Thanksgiving, and my life has been forever changed. I felt cheated because I didn't get to say good-bye, and I felt lost because a critical part of who I am no longer existed in my presence, and to be honest I just wanted to give up. But I couldn't. Even though my mom stopped breathing, I had to find the strength to keep breathing; even when the pain seemed so strong that it could snatch my breath away.

From year to year, I went through all of the emotions that losing a loved one can cause; sadness, confusion, guilt, disappointment, denial, frustration, and finally learning to cope without her being here. The coping part took me years to master because before you can ever learn to cope, healing has to happen. But how can healing happen when it is hidden under so many hurtful feelings?

As I look back on my experience of my mother passing, I feel extremely blessed to have been inspired to write this book. I wanted to write this book from a place of understanding, from a place of addressing real feelings and emotions that we face, and from a holistic perspective. Holistic simply means mind, body, and spirit. To effectively heal, we must address every part of us that is affected by the loss of Mom.

When my mom first passed away, I couldn't imagine that one day God would use my painful experience to help inspire and encourage others. This book is proof that you can triumph after tragedy.

This book is not just an informational book or an inspirational book, but I pray that it will be a source of healing and restoration for those who are hurting from their mom passing away. I personally know that it doesn't matter how long your mother has been out of your physical presence; time stands still when she is no longer with you. I remember someone asking me, "How long does it take to get over losing your mother?" From my perspective you never "get over" your mom passing away. You simply learn how to cope with her not being a physical part of your life. You learn how to keep going when you want to quit. You learn how to live when you feel like you are dying inside. You learn how to smile through the storms, and you learn how to let her life over shadow her death.

When I think about my mom not being here on earth with me, it still hurts like salt being poured into an open wound. I have mastered focusing on the good memories and the good times. But it is still difficult, especially when something amazing happens in my life, my children's lives, or my grandchildren's lives. I want to share things with her and it hurts when I can't. But one thing I know is that I have to stay strong and keep going, and so do you. Moving through life without Mom can be very difficult, but it has to be done.

I am not going to tell you I never feel numb. I

am not going to tell you there are times where I don't miss my mom like crazy, and I am not going to tell you that I am some super spiritual being that has no emotions connected to my mom passing, because none of that would be true. But I will tell you that through a loving family, amazing friends, and the power of God I am standing strong, and I have discovered my purpose on the other side of pain. I am a firm believer that where we are going to is greater than what we are going through. And that is one of the things that has kept me going and keeps me going.

I know my life would have been much different when my mom passed if I had a resource like this. It would have helped me tremendously to receive inspiration and encouragement from someone who truly understood my pain, from someone who has been there, from someone who was going to tell me, "It's okay to be mad, hurt, angry, and disappointed, but one day you will heal and be restored, so be mad at the world, but when you are finished being mad...be better."

I pray that this book touches your heart and soul in a very special way, and I hope you find yourself stronger after you complete it. This book is not meant to take away anything you are going through. It is a resource to help you find strength and healing on your journey of *Making It Without Mom.* Is there life after loss? Absolutely. So I want you to decide that you will continue to live, and not let your mom's death, be the death of you. It is okay to be sad and mourn, but at some point it is critical that you bring your life back into focus. Just imagine what your mom would want. Wouldn't she want you to move on and find healing and happiness? So are you ready? Because now is your moment to take the next step of faith toward healing. You can do it.

I am not going to say that things are going to get better overnight, because healing and restoration takes time, but what I will tell you is that making the choice to move toward healing and restoration is critical for you. You should feel extremely proud of yourself right now, because you have made a powerful choice to be better and live better, and that is something you deserve.

It is important for you to believe that you can be happy again, that you can enjoy life again, that you can effectively deal with your emotions, and that you can move forward. There is a great chance that you have more strength than you give yourself credit for. You are strong, and you are going to continue to make it today, tomorrow, and in the days to come. It's your time to be more, do more, and live more. If you have not begun the healing and restoration process, you are way overdue. This is your moment for healing, and this is your moment for restoration.

This can be the first day of the best days of the rest of your life. The best is still yet to come for you, no matter what you have been through or are going through. A journey of healing begins with the first step. As you take the first step forward, may you continue to take more and more steps that will help you become stronger and stronger with each passing day.

CHAPTER 1

Getting Over Guilt

Often as surviving children, we might feel some level of guilt that is connected to our moms passing away. I felt guilty because I was a nurse and I should have somehow known that my mother was going to pass away. I felt guilty because I didn't stop by my mother's house that Saturday morning like I usually did on Saturdays (to make sure she didn't have to get out the house in the cold to buy a Saturday paper).

I felt guilty because I didn't spend more time with her when I saw her last (even though we always spent quality time together). I felt guilty because of the money I borrowed when I was 18 that I never paid back. I felt guilty because when I was a teenager

I stayed out later than I was supposed to, and so on, and so on. You know one of the amazing things about our loving moms? They loved us, and they knew we loved them. Don't let guilt block your healing and restoration process, because it can and it will. Guilt causes your life to be on pause, and how can you move forward if your life is on pause?

Sure, there is always something that we can feel guilty about, but you can't let guilt take over your life. Guilt will consume you and can prolong the healing and restoration process. If you feel any level of guilt, you must let go of the guilt and forgive yourself, and you must do it now. Find someone to talk to, and even work with a professional counselor if you have to. Never be ashamed of your emotions because you must get over the guilt, so that might mean sharing your feelings with someone else.

Don't cut your own life short by letting it be consumed with guilt. Unaddressed guilt can turn into stress and depression. You must be sure to take care of yourself mentally, physically, emotionally, and spiritually. So part of taking care of yourself means letting go of guilt. Guilt is not something you can hold on to if you are working on healing and restoration.

And you know what? Regardless of how great of a child you were to your mom, you are always probably going to think you could have said, "I love you more," hugged her more, and spent more time with her. When she is gone, even if you said, "I love you," to her a million times, or gave her a million hugs, it is still not going to seem like enough. But the thing about love is that when you truly love someone the love and hugs are still working even when you are not actively saying it or doing it. Love is in the heart, and since it is in the heart it never stops. So even when you weren't saying I love you to your mom, and even when you weren't hugging her, your love was still flowing through her heart like a river, so she felt it every day. Mother and child are connected in a special way through the heart and soul, and it is a bond that is never broken, not even through death.

Often when a mom passes away there are things that the children feel were left unsaid, and questions left unanswered. This can prevent you from moving on. This doesn't have to be your story. Refuse to allow any type of guilt to block you from moving forward. Healthy grief releases guilt and doesn't hold on to it. Guilt can keep you stuck in grief and locked in the past, which is not beneficial for your life, or joy.

CHAPTER 2

Letting The Breath Of God Heal and Restore You

People told me don't question God, and don't be upset with God. Well, I had questions, and I was upset with God. I didn't understand why my mother who was so full of life had to die. I didn't understand why my children had to be left without a grandmother that they adored, and I didn't understand why some people who didn't appreciate their mothers still had theirs, and I didn't have mine.

I didn't understand why my kind, loving mom, the one who loved unconditionally and would do anything for anybody, loved God to the fullest and was a perfect example of someone with a Christ-like heart and attitude, had to die in her yard alone on a cold winter day. Why didn't God put it on my heart to go by my mom's house that morning instead of going shopping? Why did God not help her? After all, He is God right? All of those questions consumed my mind. It was easy to blame God. But even when everything seems out of control, God is still in control, so don't feel helpless or hopeless. God has a blueprint for healing and His Word is that blueprint. It is a guide for not only healing but restoration as well.

Yes, I was mad, sad, hurt, and confused. Sometimes people are not honest enough when they go through pain related to the loss of their mom. They say, "I wasn't angry at God. I trusted Him, and I knew Mom was in a better place." Well for me, that wasn't realistic. My mother was 51 years old and full of life, and I felt mad, angry, and upset with God. We have to be honest if we are angry with God. We don't have to act like we have it all together or that we are not angry or confused with God. The reason I say that is because it is important to be honest if you are angry with God. Because if you don't acknowledge being angry at God, how can you heal from it? How can you develop a closer relationship with someone you are consistently angry and mad at?

What usually happens when we are angry and upset with someone is that we grow distant from them and not closer. So being honest about any angry feelings toward God is important. Acknowledge those feelings and work through them. Do faith-building things that will increase your faith in God and His Word. What happens many times is that people get angry and upset with God, and they stay that way for the rest of their lives. They grow distant from God and never experience the true and unconditional love He has for them.

The reality is that God's love has tremendous healing power. The more you understand God's love, the better you can feel, and when you feel better you will respond to your pain differently. God's love can heal a hurting heart and fully restore you. And no matter how big your pain is, God's love and power is bigger. Sometimes in the midst of pain it might be hard to feel God's love, but He is there with you. He will never leave you. So remember you are not going through the loss of your mom with God being absent.

Release all of your pain into God's hands because it is now your time to experience joy and peace and to move forward. God will wrap His loving arms around you and give you joy, peace, comfort, strength, and even understanding. Never back down from pain;

face it with faith. Many times we try everything else to help us through pain, only to feel the same or maybe even worse. But true healing and restoration is only found through God because God's love and power can reach places that other things can't.

Now, even though I was mad at God, I never backed away from my faith. Why? Because I knew that my outcome of learning how to make it without mom would be better with God than without Him. Being upset with God never caused me to approach Him in a way that was out of character for me, and I never cursed God. I never told God I hate Him, but I was angry. I quickly learned that even if I was mad at God not to stay mad at him, because I was going to need Him for something else in my life.

I thought that because I had a close relationship with God that meant I would be exempt from going through painful things. For some reason, I thought because I was honoring God with my life I would not go through anything so hurtful like my mom passing away. I felt like I had a special plan of protection that Christians get because you belong to God. So I was shocked and confused when I realized that wasn't the case. I even created a checklist in my head of what I did wrong, or what I could have done better, so that God would not be mad at me. It took a lot of faith for me to realize that God didn't abandon me, and He would see me through.

Sometimes during the pain, it seems like God doesn't hear your prayers. It seems like all of the yelling and crying doesn't get His attention. But God cares, and He will help you. So stay connected to your spiritual source of healing and strength. Fuel yourself with faith and be determined to get stronger.

Being fueled by faith is essential to healing and restoration. That means you don't have to do things on your own. There are many things you can do to build your faith like go to church consistently, listen to faith-filled messages, have a spiritual support system, read books that build your faith, have a strong prayer life, and keep the Word of God alive in you.

Even if you have to, find one scripture and read it every day, or several times a day. Get it deep down in your heart, and soul, and let it guide you toward healing and restoration. I put my healing scriptures on index cards, and I kept them in my purse, so they would be with me wherever I went. And yes, they did give me strength.

Sometimes I would read the scriptures or say them with tears running down my face, and with barely enough strength to hold my head up. But after staying consistent one day I realized that the scriptures were a daily part of my healing and restoration plan. And when I stopped reading my cards every day, as soon as I felt a sad Mom moment coming on, the scriptures would kick in automatically. They became embedded in my heart and soul.

CHAPTER 3

Letting Your Mom's Life Overshadow Her Death

Letting your mom's life overshadow her death is one of the best ways to release grief. Every day that you wake up, you choose your behaviors. That also means you choose your mental behaviors. You can decide if you are going to have disempowering and hurtful thoughts or empowering and happy thoughts. I know that having happy thoughts in the midst of so much pain can seem impossible. But effectively using your mind is critical to healing and restoration.

You can still have peace in the midst of pain when you focus on healing and not pain. If you constantly focus on the pain, that's where you will remain, but when you release the pain you can move forward. Because whatever you continue to focus on gets bigger, and what you continue to focus on you maximize. So if you continue to focus on the pain, you maximize it, but if you continue to focus on healing, you maximize that. And that is what you will attract into your life. Focus on God's promise of healing even when you are hurting, and you can find yourself getting stronger and stronger with each day that passes.

Healing is something you and God go through together, but it takes faith as well as action, so there are some things you can do from your end. You have to consciously be aware of your thoughts, words, and actions. You have to ask yourself, "Is this thought, word, or action moving me toward healing and restoration or away from healing and restoration?" And if they are not moving you forward, you have to immediately replace the wrong thought, words, or action with the right ones.

Remember, you have to make sure your thoughts, words, and actions are working in alignment with the healing process, and not against it. This might take a little time, but with dedication it can become a way of life for you, and that can bring you a greater level of happiness and healing. What you focus on you get more of, so focusing on the right thing is extremely important for healing and restoration. Focusing on good feelings will manifest more of them. When you feel down, shift to a memory of your mom that makes you smile, feel joyful, positive, and motivated. Refocusing your energy toward things that are positive is a great piece of the healing and restoration puzzle.

Since we have the power to choose what we think about. It is never a good idea to keep replaying all of the painful events connected to your mom passing. As I mentioned before, that is one of the things I used to do, and it caused me years and years of additional grief. I just didn't know how to break free from the thoughts that were robbing me of my joy and peace. It wasn't until I learned how to replace the wrong way of thinking with the right way of thinking that I began to heal.

Now, that doesn't mean you can't think of your mom, but what it does means is that you have to be careful about what you are thinking about. If you constantly replay your mom's last moments over and over, or if you constantly think about the not so good times connected with her passing, then it can cause you to spiral down into an emotional slump, one that is extremely hard to get out of. Trust me I know, that happened to me.

For a long time, I didn't realize that I had authority over my thoughts. So since I had dominion over my thoughts, that meant I could focus on things that made me smile, and not cry...well, not cry as much. And since I had authority over my thoughts, that meant I could control my thoughts and not let them control me. Not controlling my thoughts meant that I was possibly opening myself up to stress and depression. Now, it is important to understand that it is okay to feel sad, but when the sadness is transforming into grief related stress and depression, that is where the problem comes in at. So it is important to immediately replace any thoughts that are not helping to bring out the best in you with thoughts that are.

And this is where letting your mom's life overshadow her death comes in at. It is important to know that the right thoughts can move you closer to healing, or farther away from healing. It is important to think thoughts about your mom that are good thoughts, and not depressing thoughts. It is essential to celebrate the beautiful days of her life, and not the sad memory of her death. Focus on the amazing person your mom was, focus on the good times you spent together, focus on the times she laughed, the hugs, the love, and the joyful moments. Focus on the times when you were growing up that are beautiful memories. This is a shift in thinking that can help with inner healing and peace.

A positive and optimistic attitude helps to fuel the healing and restoration process. This not only includes positive thinking, but it also includes positive language. What you think you speak, and the more you believe it, the more you say it, and the more you give power to it. So it is important to think healing thoughts and speak healing words. They work together.

Every morning you can say, "I am going to have a sad day," or you can say, "I am going to think of one thing to be thankful for today, and have an amazing day, to the best of my ability." Sad and painful words equal a sad and painful image, and you want to create an image that guides you toward healing and restoration.

CHAPTER 4

How to Survive the Holiday Season Without Mom

Every day without mom is difficult, but the holiday season can be extremely challenging emotionally. The holiday season was always hard for me for many reasons. For one my mom passed away during the holiday season, her memorial service was during the holiday season, the holidays were always so special to her, and she made the holidays so fun and exciting. After she passed the holiday season just didn't seem the same for me, and it still isn't. But I have learned how to make it through the holiday season without her and enjoy the family I am blessed to

21

have left.

Not seeing my mom at holiday family functions was extremely difficult, and I still miss her presence a lot, but learning how to survive the holiday season without her has made all of the difference for me emotionally. I am going to provide you with 35 tips on how to survive the holiday season without Mom. Of course, these are not the only 35 tips that can help you, but this list can be a great resource to help you.

1.   Celebrate your mom's life in a unique way during the holiday season.

2.   Look for daily inspiration.

3.   Help others during the holiday season (This can help you to find joy and peace).

4.   Do whatever you need to do to make the holiday season bright.

5. Make extra room for happiness during the holiday season.

6. Fill your day with peace.

7. Wake up daily with an uplifting attitude and maintain it throughout the day.

8. Read material that will help you feel encouraged.

9. Do things that will add joy to your life.

10. Carry a winner's attitude with you throughout the day.

11. Find ways to keep your spirits lifted during the holiday season.

12. If you do find yourself having an emotional setback try to bounce back quickly.

13. Holiday depression is real, so talk with a counselor or someone that specializes in holiday grief if you need to.

14. Recall positive memories of your mom during the holiday season.

15. Make your mom's favorite dish or do something else to help you feel like she is still a special part of the holiday season.

16. Each day, find time for laughter even in the midst of the tears.

17. You might have a reason to feel sad during the holiday season, but you also have many reasons to smile. Find at least one reason to smile and let it carry you through the holiday season.

18. Accept the realization that you are going to miss your mom, but also know that even though it is hard, you can make it through the holiday season without her.

19. Share your holiday childhood memories with others.

20. Believe that you can make it through the holiday season.

21. Listen to uplifting music that makes you feel amazing and happy on the inside.

22. Have a strategy for survival before the holiday season hits.

23. Think positive.

24. Speak positive.

25. Donate to a charity in honor of your mom to help someone else during the holiday season.

26. Lean on family and friends for strength (It's okay to share your pain with those who understand, are compassionate and care). Don't feel like you have to go through it alone.

27. Look at pictures if that makes you feel strengthened.

28. Find something about the holiday season that you look forward to.

29. Buy a beautiful flower and let it serve as a symbol as a special tribute to your mom during the holiday season.

30. Celebrate the holiday season with your loved ones and create priceless memories for the future.

31. You can write a poem and keep a journal; writing can help the healing process. Create a poem and post it online. Your poem may help to inspire someone else to heal.

32. Make a memorial journal of your mom with her pictures, favorite quotes, and a poem. This should not look like a shrine that can cause depression but this should be something that

brings joy and makes you smile. It should be something that inspires you.

33. Take it day by day and celebrate the good days, and strive to make the not so good days better.

34. Be grateful for the people you are still blessed to have in your life. Be thankful for everything, the things you can see, and the things you can't see (like joy, peace, strength).

35. Every day when you wake up, and every night before you go to bed, hold in your mind the things you have to be thankful for (you can even make a daily list, and keep it where you can see it several times a day, if this helps).

CHAPTER 5

The Mom Legacy

It is important to continue to honor the life of your mother. What if she could peek into your life right now? What would she want to see? What would make her smile? What would make her proud of you? What would bring her joy? Those are the things you can do to honor your mom's life and her legacy.

I realized that my mom will never die. She will always be in me. I am who I am because of her. Your mom may not be physically here on earth anymore, but she is still with you in your heart and soul. Her life is still breathing through the amazing legacy that she has left behind. And as her child, you are part of her beautiful legacy. When you let your mom's legacy

29

shine through you that is a pathway to healing and restoration. Memories of your mom can guide you through the hurt .

Even when Mom is no longer here on earth her legacy is. And her legacy is something that can continue to live on. The mom legacy should be like a wet footprint in cement that has dried. It should leave a lasting imprint for generations to come.

As children, we all have a piece of Mom in us. For me, it is my mom's inspirational and encouraging nature, her kind heart, and her spirit of giving. My mom also left the legacy of accomplishment, and faith as well. Essential things that our mothers leave are not just tangible, but they are also things that are intangible as well. It is up to us as children to continue to share the legacy of our mothers. Think about the amazing legacy your mother left. Isn't that such a beautiful feeling? When I think about the legacy of my mother, it is like she has breathed encouragement into my soul.

One day it dawned on me that when we have tragedies in our lives there are only two ways that they can affect us. They can either tear us down or build us up. At that moment, I decided to let my mom's passing build me up. After all, that is what she would have wanted. I became involved in a ministry group where many times I was able to speak to women and share my story and help encourage them to keep the faith. I sponsored a banquet in my mom's name helping high school students. I wrote spiritual poetry in her honor, and I live in her honor.

I decided to grab my pain by the throat and conquer it. I decided to let my mom's death give me life. And still to this day I speak about my mom and what

31

I went through emotionally when she passed away, and it is amazing that years later I am still able to help others by sharing my story. And I feel like, as long I continued to carry on my mom's legacy, I will continue to feel lifted and not torn down.

How can you keep your mom's memory ongoing, and let her impactful legacy continue to shine bright? You have what it takes to carry on the vision and legacy of your mom and to keep her memory alive.

CHAPTER 6

Kitchen Table Conversations With Mom

Most of us have probably had a conversation with Mom at the kitchen table, whether it was when we were growing up, at a family gathering, or even just those special times when we sat at the table and chatted with her, while she fixed a meal, baked a dessert, or was just relaxing.

One of the things that helps my family and I stay strong is to think about what my mom said when encouragement, inspiration, or support was needed. This may help you also. It is true that our moms may not be here physically but their encouraging and loving words will never die; they still have life, and they can continue to make us feel full of life.

I learned many, many life lessons from my mom, like unconditional love, how to have relentless dedication to my dreams, how to have unwavering faith, how to be a great mom, grandmother and more. The life lessons that your mom taught you are lessons that you could never learn in a classroom. They are lessons that she learned through wisdom from living life. Life lessons from mom are the best lessons I have ever been taught. Cherish everything that your mom taught you, and hold those things close to your heart. That is something that will never fade away.

Spiritual Mom Hugs:

When you feel down and discouraged, a spiritual mom hug can help. What is a spiritual mom hug? A spiritual mom hug is the love you still feel from your mom, even though she is no longer in your presence. When you need an encouraging word from mom, or a spiritual mom hug, imagine one of those kitchen table talks. This can be beneficial when you are feeling pain, feeling sad, having a problem, or just need to think of Mom and smile. Focus on what your mom would say and allow her loving response to flow through your heart and soul. You can write down the encouraging words that your mom might say, or once said, to you. This can help you to feel better.

As children, this should not be difficult at all. Most of us know exactly what our moms would say to us when we need to be lifted. Now you have to be honest when you are writing down words she would say. If your mom would tell you to get your rear in gear, then be real in capturing the essence of her personality. That is going to make it feel authentic to you.

You can keep a WOW (Words Of Wisdom) Mom Journal. This is where you write down some of the words of wisdom that your mom spoke to you. You can write them on index cards, put them in a small photo album, and put her picture in the front. This can not only inspire you, but other family members as well. You can look at it often for inspiration and encouragement. You can also include other things like your mom's favorite quotes, hobbies, and other things to help you positively remember your mom.

You can also write an encouraging letter to yourself and think about what your mom would say. Keep this letter somewhere where you can see it often. You can use this as a source of inspiration and motivation. Any favorite memories about your mom and any life lessons she has taught you, can help you as you continue to move toward healing and restoration.

CHAPTER 7

Have A Strong Support System

I can honestly say that without a strong support system I would have completely fallen apart. You don't have to go through the loss of your mom alone; your support system is there for strength, support, and guidance. The people in your corner will not just allow you to go through learning how to cope with the loss of your mom, but they will go through it with you.

I did feel like 99% of me was an emotional mess after my mom passed, but it was that 1% that I held on to. It was that 1% that my support system helped me to build upon to become better, and it was that 1% that helped me to become who I am today. You should always have someone in place that you can talk to. Don't just sit in the house in a dark room, and feel sad, and shut everyone out of your world. That is something that I found myself doing, but my support system wasn't having it. And I am so glad about that. I am truly grateful for them all today; because if it wasn't for my support system my outcome would have been much different. Yes, God is there spiritually, but you also need people there for you in the physical realm.

One of the worst things you can do is seclude yourself from those who care about you. Remember they care for you, and it probably hurts them deeply to know that you are hurting so badly. Just like you want the best for your life, so do they. So don't disconnect yourself from your support system. Stay connected to them. You don't want to create bad vibes between you and your support system, not only because they don't deserve it, but what is going to happen as you reach a healthy point of healing and restoration? The last thing you want is to have to deal with is another painful loss because you have turned your support system away by shutting them out of your life. So even through the pain, stay close to those who are on the journey of healing and restoration with you. In the end, you will be happy that you did.

And don't stop doing things you were doing with your family and friends. This doesn't mean that you are 100% happy, but what it does mean is that you understand that you still have to put yourself in an atmosphere of positivity that will help to facilitate your healing and restoration. And if you are not used to spending a lot of time with family and friends then start. Even if you have to choose one day out of the week that you get together with someone from your support system, do it. This will help you to stay motivated, and it will help you to create beautiful memories with those who are important to you.

We have to take the opportunity to spend time with those who are special to us while we are blessed with the opportunity. You don't have to spend hours with them at first if you don't want to. If it is better for you to take small steps, then start with 30 minutes a week and add time as you continue to move forward. The key is to maintain connection with your support system.

Your support system will love you even when you are appearing unlovable. They won't let a bad attitude or bad emotions affect their dedication to you, and they love you unconditionally, through the good times and through the not so good times. Your support system should come close to you, and not pull away. And even if it feels like they are pulling away, that probably is not the case. Sometimes even those closest to you don't know what to say when you are coping with such a difficult loss. So it is important to let them know that it is okay not to know what to say.

I lost many people out of my life during the time my mom passed away simply because they didn't know what to say to me, which made them uncomfortable being around me. And that put hurt on top of hurt. Your support system needs to understand that this is new for them, and it's also new for you. So anything they can do to support you and help you to stay strong is welcome.

Now on the flip side of that is that your support system also needs to challenge you when you need to be challenged. Now this might not sound appropriate, but it is. If someone cares about you and they see you drowning in pain, part of being a great support person is for them to help pull you out of the pain and not to help you sink. So when people are giving you caring, loving advice, it is important to listen. And the caring and loving advice should only provide positive encouragement; this should not be a way of communicating that is demeaning, belittling, or non- caring. It should still be delivered in a loving manner. Their words should comfort and empower you.

I can look back and see when my support people used tough love with me. At the time, it didn't feel too good, but now it feels great because it helped me to heal. It helped me to stay in the victor, and not victim mindset, and it helped me to get out and stay out of a way of thinking, speaking, and acting that was going against my healing and restoration.

And don't be afraid to get close to people again, or stay close to people, for fear that they might pass away. That is no way to live your life. I also dealt with that. You just have to love the ones you have in your life to the fullest while they are here. Enjoy spending time with them while you can, and create as many priceless memories as possible.

CHAPTER 8

Getting Back to The Best Of You

Making it without mom seems like a pain that will never heal, I have been there, and I want to let you know that things will get better if you allow them to, and if you believe they will. A mom passing can cause emotional and physical scars that can last a lifetime. But whatever you do, don't let the pain steal you from you. Remember who you were before your mom passed. You must refuse to let the pain from the past define your present. It is time for you to make the ultimate life comeback. Even when you are hurting you still have to be dedicated to being the best expression of yourself that you can be.

When you are going through pain due to the loss of your mom, it is so easy for you to get lost in the midst of pain. But it is important for you to continue to take care of you. And it is not just about taking care of yourself on the inside, but it is also about taking care of yourself on the outside too. One of the things I absolutely love that my mom used to say is, "Just because you are going through something, doesn't mean you have to look like it."

Even though you may have a lot of pain on the inside, take care of your outside. That will help you with the healing and restoration process. When you look in the mirror, your reflection should not show that you are going through one of the worst storms of your life. Your reflection should show that you are victorious, that you are going to make it, and that you are an overcomer. It is so easy to wear our pain, because what is going on the inside of us can show up on the outside of us, but you have to be dedicated to not neglect yourself in the process of healing and restoration.

Continue to do things that will help you feel better from within. For example meditating, taking walks, relaxing, eating healthy, and other things specific for you and your lifestyle. These things will help you to continue to take care of yourself. One of the things I dealt with when my mom passed was emotional eating. I ate for comfort, and because I was feeling stressed. I had to realize that type of behavior wasn't contributing to me being the best me I could be. I had to learn how to stay focused on behaviors that were going to benefit me.

Going through the loss of a mom can easily trigger stress, emotional eating, and other behaviors and unhealthy habits that can block you from taking care of you. So become dedicated to doing things that are best for you mind, body, and spirit. You have already lost your mom; don't lose yourself, too. As I discussed previously, you must be the way your mom would want you to be. So any habits or behaviors that are not bringing the best out of you, means that you are not taking care of yourself the way you should be. There are a lot of people who love and care for you, and they don't want to see you lose focus of the amazing, phenomenal, victorious person you are. So do whatever you need to do to take care of you. Your mom was important, and so are you.

And as you are getting back to the best of you, what about also unveiling a new you? This doesn't mean that you totally forget about who you were before your mom passed, but what it means is that you are going to bounce back better than ever. It also means that you are going to have a renewed sense of joy, peace, and purpose.

Being made new means that you are revitalized from the inside-out, and it is in a sense creating a brand new version of you...a happier and more fulfilled version of yourself. Why? Because once you begin to heal from the passing of your mom, something new is released in you that can make you feel like you are stronger than you ever were.

When I think back to the person I was before my mom passed, I was strong, but not as nearly as strong as I am today. I had the heart to encourage others, but not anywhere near like I do today. I loved and cherished those who meant a lot to me, but not nearly as much as I do today. So even though I am still me, I am the best version of myself that I can be, and you also

49

must become dedicated to becoming the best you that you can be. What does that look like for you? Think about how you can become the best version of yourself that you can be, and then take action to become that person.

CHAPTER 9

Knowing Your Emotional Pain Triggers and Not Going Back

It is easy to go back to the past and dig up all of the pain, but you must make a decision that you are going to keep moving forward. It is important for you to continue to implement things in your life that will help you rise above the pain of losing your mom.

A part of continuing to move forward is not allowing emotional pain triggers to hold you back from healing and restoration. If you don't recognize your emotional pain triggers, the pain will seep back in through the cracks in your mind and spirit, and can hinder you with reclaiming your power over pain. Emotional pain triggers can also cause you to become depressed and stuck.

One of my emotional pain triggers used to be pictures. I couldn't look at a picture of my mom without falling back into an emotional rut. Now that might not be your story; each individual is different. That is why it is important to know your specific emotional pain triggers. Know what you can handle emotionally and what causes emotional setbacks for you. Today, I can look at my mom's picture and do just fine, but it took the process of healing and restoration for me to be strengthened when it came to looking at my mom's picture.

I used to constantly read my mom's obituary as well, and that was also another emotional pain trigger for me. Another thing I did was constantly reflect on the day she passed over and over and over. None of those things were helping me to heal; they were all emotional pain triggers that were causing me to move backwards instead of forward. It is important to recognize what has the potential to delay your healing process. Those are blocks to your restoration. And don't feel bad if you have emotional pain triggers, or if another family member is able to do something and it doesn't have the same emotional impact on them that it has on you. That is okay. Just like what happened for me, there is a great chance that one day your emotional pain triggers will become easier, too.

You have to create a list of pain triggers that are specific for you. Your pain triggers are anything you notice causing pain that sets you back and stops you from becoming stronger.

CHAPTER 10

You Have Purpose On The Other Side Of Pain

You only have one chance here on earth to live life fulfilled and with purpose. That is something you deserve. Your purpose is why you were birthed on earth. It is not just what you are meant to do, but also who you were created to be. Pain has a way of overshadowing your purpose and making you feel like it doesn't even exist. But it is important to realize that regardless of the pain you go through, God has purpose for you. Just knowing that you have purpose can be huge when it comes to healing and restoration. For so long, I allowed pain to cast a cloud over my purpose, but today I can say I am free, happy, and purpose filled. God has a way of putting all of the pieces of pain together, and they end up being purposeful.

Death does not have the victory, you do. On the other side of going through is coming out. And believe it or not, you can come out better than when you went in. You can come out with more power, strength, wisdom, compassion, drive, and purpose.

Don't let the past identify who you are. You are not your pain. You are going through the pain, but don't stop there and let it shape your life in a negative non-fulfilling way. Either you are going to overcome the pain or let it overcome you. And when pain overcomes you, it consumes you mentally, emotionally, spiritually, and physically. It strips you of your identity, takes over your life and keeps you living in the past instead of moving forward. You can take charge of your life, and you can do it now. Make the decision that you are going to do something to transform your pain into purpose, and then do it. It is all about choices and action. It is all about rising above the pain with purpose.

Even though your mom is no longer here on earth, you still have purpose on this earth. Yes, God can take your greatest pain, and transform it into purpose. A lot of ministries, businesses, books, plays, and other things were birthed out of pain.

Get a picture in your mind of yourself healed and restored and move toward that picture. Do what you need to do to get better and live better. The mending process has begun in my life, and I love it. I am living my life to the fullest. I have persevered through the hardest times in my life. I have had some storms, and now I am beginning to see the rainbow. I feel restored and mended. That is not to say that I won't go

through any more storms in my life, but I am con-
fident that now I know how to successfully make it
through them.

No one said that making it without mom would
be easy, but with faith in God, determination and inner strength it is possible. Just think back to a time
when you were faced with storms. Once you were
blessed to make it through them, you were probably
stronger and you probably felt more victorious. There
is something about making it through something with
God that empowers you in a way that words can't describe. Turn your pain over to God and watch Him see
you through and bring you out, greater than you can
even imagine.

Losing your mom can knock you down, but you
have to not only get back up, you have to get back up
better than when you were when you were knocked

down. You have to get back up stronger, more determined to succeed, and more powerful.

Sometimes when we go through the tragic experience of losing a mom, it can make us feel empty and
like our own life has no meaning. It can rob us of our
purpose and vision, so it is important to know that
being in pain does not give you permission to give up.
I know that sometimes the fog of pain is so thick that
we can't see through it, but even through the fog of
pain there is meaning and purpose. Your brightest
days are still in front of you, and with God by your
side, things will get better. God's love and power pro-
vides strength, hope, and healing. God can cause your
pain to work in a powerful way that not only helps
you to press through the pain, but through your story of survival you can also help others press through
their pain too.

A harsh realization for me was that time was not going to stand still and wait on me to heal, and I was losing precious time that I could never get back. Moving through the pain is one of the hardest yet necessary things to do. You might have to start slow, and take one step at a time, but you must move past the pain. If you don't the pain will paralyze you mentally, emotionally, and spiritually, and it will block you from moving forward. There is no right way or wrong way to move past the pain. Just find something that works for you that will positively move you forward. Let the beautiful memory of your mom be the wind beneath your wings that gently blows you forward.

Your pain can be a motivator. It can actually push you toward your purpose. I will use myself for example. I have been blessed to launch successful businesses to inspire others, I have spoken at times and shared my testimony regarding my mother, and how I found my purpose in the midst of pain, and I was blessed to write this book. Those are all examples of transforming pain into purpose.

What can you do in the next six months to live the whole and abundant life that you desire and deserve? If you continue to live in pain then you give energy to the wrong things. You want to give your energy to the right things, the things that are going to help your life come back into focus, the things that are going to restore your joy and happiness, and the things that are going to serve your life in a meaningful way. Now, your life may never be restored to the level that it was before you mom passed away, but you can have a new found type of life renewal. That unleashes a new you. It is possible because it happened for me.

Conclusion

Thank you for purchasing this book. I hope that it inspired and encouraged you in a very special way. At first, when God inspired me to write this book, honestly, I wasn't excited, not because I didn't want to help others, but because I thought it would open up too much pain, but instead I found the strength to write, and now that this book is finished it helped me more than I realized.

I feel extremely blessed to have been inspired to write this book, and I am so grateful to God. I have learned to celebrate my mom's new life in heaven and go on with my life in a new and powerful way. As difficult as it is on some days, I am stronger than I have ever been. And I have continued to gain strength, as I celebrate my mom's new life in heaven and not grieve over her loss here on earth.

I made it, and you are going to make it, too. Today you are okay. You are not *going to be* okay; you are already okay. Just believe it, and keep moving forward. And remember that you can heal and recover from the pain of losing your mom. You are more than a survivor, you are a conqueror. So remain dedicated to getting stronger day by day, and know that I believe in you and your ability to continue to reclaim your power over pain.

About The Author

D r. Shauntel Peak-Jimenez is an Author, Certified Life Coach, Certified Business Coach, and a Certified Life Coach Trainer. She is also a nurse, and she has earned a Bachelor of Arts in Psychology, a Master of Arts in Biblical Studies, and a Doctorate in Christian Counseling. She is currently pursuing a

Doctorate in Philosophy, with an emphasis in Holistic Life Coaching.

Dr. Shauntel Peak-Jimenez is also a Certified Law of Attraction Practitioner, and a Certified Neuro-Linguistic Programming (NLP) Practitioner. She has also completed numerous other certification programs. She is dedicated to continuous learning in the areas of personal and professional development.

Dr. Shauntel Peak-Jimenez has a passion to write, and she has empowered thousands through her online articles. Her life mission is to help others live their best life possible. She has a gift to help individuals break through obstacles and challenges, and achieve their goals and dreams. She feels blessed to help others excel to levels of greatness.

At one point in her life, Dr. Shauntel Peak-Jimenez was single mother of five living on welfare.

But over 20 years ago, she decided that she needed to shift her life in a different direction. She encountered adversity after adversity but persevered to accomplish phenomenal achievements academically, personally, and professionally. She faced many emotional struggles after the unexpected passing of her mother in 2001. She feels blessed to have been restored emotionally and spiritually, and she is dedicated to encouraging others to find hope in the midst of pain too.

Made in the USA
Las Vegas, NV
08 March 2022

45246020R00059